NOODLES

NOODLES

Queen Street House
4 Queen Street
Bath BA1 1HE, UK

ISBN: 978-1-4454-0704-3

Printed in China

Internal design by Fiona Roberts
Produced by the Bridgewater Book Company Ltd
Photography by David Jordan
Home economy by Jacqueline Bellefontaine

Notes for the Reader

This book uses imperial, metric, and US cup measurements. Follow the same units of
measurement throughout; do not mix imperial and metric. All spoon measurements are
level: teaspoons are assumed to be 5 ml, and tablespoons are assumed to be 15 ml. Unless
otherwise stated, milk is assumed to be whole, eggs and individual vegetables such as
potatoes are medium, and pepper is freshly ground black pepper.

The times given are an approximate guide only. Preparation times differ according to the
techniques used by different people and the cooking times may also vary from those given
as a result of the type of oven used. Optional ingredients, variations or serving suggestions
have not been included in the calculations.

Recipes using raw or very lightly cooked eggs should be avoided by infants, the elderly,
pregnant women, convalescents, and anyone with a chronic condition. Pregnant and
breastfeeding women are advised to avoid eating peanuts and peanut products. Sufferers
from nut allergies should be aware that some of the ready-prepared ingredients used in the
recipes in this book may contain nuts. Always check the packaging before use.

Front cover image: Fettuccine with asparagus and prosciutto © Dennis Gottlieb/Getty Images

Introduction

ASIAN NOODLES WILL DELIGHT YOU AND EVERYONE YOU COOK FOR. THESE SIMPLE INGREDIENTS CAN BE MADE INTO SOPHISTICATED OR INFORMAL MEALS TO SUIT ALL LIFESTYLES, AND OFFER A FANTASTIC ARRAY OF PALATE-TINGLING FLAVORS.

A VAST VARIETY OF NOODLES EXISTS IN ASIA, BUT ONLY A SELECTION IS READILY AVAILABLE IN THE WEST. THESE RECIPES FEATURE NOODLES THAT YOU CAN BUY IN MANY SUPERMARKETS OR ASIAN AND HEALTH FOOD STORES, BUT DON'T BE PUT OFF A RECIPE BECAUSE YOU CAN'T BUY THE NOODLE SPECIFIED—ASIAN NOODLE DISHES ARE EASILY ADAPTED. EACH BRAND, HOWEVER, HAS ITS OWN PECULIARITIES SO READ THE COOKING INSTRUCTIONS BEFORE YOU START, AND CHECK WHETHER THEY ARE COOKED BEFORE THE TIME SPECIFIED ON THE LABEL. ASIAN NOODLES SHOULD BE SOFTER THAN AL DENTE ITALIAN PASTA, BUT NOT SO OVERCOOKED THAT THEY TURN TO MUSH.

Types of Noodles

HERE IS A SELECTION OF NOODLES USED IN THIS BOOK:

BUCKWHEAT NOODLES: These gray-brown noodles from Japan, sold in supermarkets and Asian food stores, are also called soba noodles. Made from buckwheat flour, they have a rectangular shape, like thin Italian taglierini. Always rinse after cooking to remove excess starch. Green tea noodles are made from both buckwheat and wheat flours.

CELLOPHANE NOODLES: Also called bean thread noodles or transparent noodles, these thin noodles are made from ground mung beans. They develop a slippery texture and glossy appearance after being soaked or boiled. Look for these in Asian food stores.

EGG NOODLES: Widely available, these are the pale yellow noodles that are commonly thought of as "Chinese noodles." Made with wheat and eggs, these are mainly sold dried, although you can find fresh egg noodles in Asian food stores. Ramen noodles are Japanese egg noodles. Egg noodles come in a variety of thicknesses and are quickly boiled.

WHEAT NOODLES: Made without eggs, fresh Hokkien noodles, from China, are thick and bright yellow. Somen are ultra-thin dried wheat noodles from Japan. Udon noodles are thick, round, and white, sold in vacuum packs or dried. Asian food stores and health food stores are the best sources for wheat noodles. If you can't find any, substitute egg noodles. Rinse well after boiling.

RICE-FLOUR NOODLES: Originally from China, rice-flour noodles feature in cuisines throughout Asia. Sold in many supermarkets, dried rice-flour noodles, made from ground rice, wheat, and water, come in a variety of thicknesses. They develop a mat, white appearance after being boiled or soaked, and are used in salads, soups, and stir-fries. The very thin rice-flour noodles are called vermicelli noodles. Medium and thick rice-flour noodles are flat, like Italian tagliatelle. These are sometimes labeled as rice sticks.

Rice-flour noodles can be cooked in boiling water for speedy preparation, but they can quickly turn to mush. The recipes in this book soak the noodles, rather than boil them, but feel free to follow package instructions, if you prefer.

Give dinner parties and drinks parties a contemporary edge with these fusion-style noodle dishes. From stylish one-bite canapés to light and delicate salads and a modern twist on a traditional soup, these recipes are the obvious choices to set the tone for a Chinese-style meal. They are equally suitable as first courses for simple suppers or drinks with friends. If you want noodle-based lunch or party food on a larger scale, simply double or triple the quantities. These recipes are versatile, light, and zingy, and will stimulate the palate for whatever is to follow. They will soon become part of your entertaining repertoire.

Jewellike cellophane noodles and other delicate, thin noodles feature in most of these recipes, but if you can't find the one specified, the more readily available egg noodles are fine.

A GOOD START WITH NOODLES

Most of the recipes in this chapter can be prepared in advance, leaving you plenty of time to entertain your guests, although a couple require your attention for last-minute cooking.

When it comes to presentation, unleash your creativity and choose whatever style you like. Large, plain white plates show off the contrast between vibrant vegetable colors and delicate noodles to best advantage, or present food on Asian-style plates and bowls for a more traditional look. If you want to go all out, many Asian food stores sell glossy, dark green fresh banana leaves, which make a stunning backdrop for noodle dishes. These recipes are so deliciously different that everybody will be impressed.

SERVES 4
1 sirloin steak, weighing about
    7 oz/200 g and ¾ inch/2 cm thick
peanut or corn oil, for brushing
salt and pepper
1 red bell pepper, cut in half, cored,
    and seeded
1 yellow bell pepper, cut in half,
    cored, and seeded
1 carrot, peeled and cut into
    3-inch/7.5-cm pieces

1 zucchini, cut into 3-inch/7.5-cm
    pieces
3½ oz/100 g canned straw
    mushrooms (drained weight),
    rinsed and thinly sliced
⅜ cup bean sprouts
2 kaffir lime leaves, sliced
2 tbsp finely chopped fresh cilantro,
    and some sprigs for garnish
3½ oz/100 g dried cellophane noodles

SWEET CHILI DRESSING
½–1 fresh red chili, to taste, seeded
    and finely sliced
4 tbsp fresh lime juice
2 tbsp rice vinegar
1 tbsp brown sugar
½ tbsp nam pla (Thai fish sauce)

Shimmering Beef Salad

Pan-fried cellophane noodles make crunchy wafers that are excellent with this salad. Heat 2 inches/5 cm oil in a wok over high heat. Pull a small bunch of noodles away from the main bunch and drop them in the hot oil. They will become crisp in seconds. Remove and drain.

• This colorful salad involves careful preparation, but fortunately all the time-consuming vegetable slicing can be done several hours in advance. Start, however, by cooking the steak. Heat a skillet over medium–high heat. Brush both sides of the steak with oil and season. Cook for 3 minutes on one side, then flip it over and continue cooking for 2 minutes for medium-rare, then set it aside for 1–2 minutes. Meanwhile, put all the ingredients for the dressing together in a large serving bowl. Thinly slice the steak on the diagonal and add to the bowl. Set aside.

• Now prepare the vegetables, adding each one to the bowl as it is sliced. You want the thinnest possible vegetable strips, so use a vegetable peeler rather than a knife. Run the peeler along the cut edges of the bell peppers to make thin, narrow strips. Thinly slice the carrot and zucchini lengthwise, then stack the slices and cut lengthwise into short thin sticks. Stir the mushrooms, bean sprouts, lime leaves, and cilantro into the dressing, then cover and let chill.

• Meanwhile, put the noodles in another bowl, pour over enough lukewarm water to cover, and let soak for 20 minutes, until soft. Alternatively, follow the package instructions. Drain and let chill until you are ready to serve.

• When you are ready to serve, toss the noodles into the salad. Arrange the salad on 4 plates and garnish with cilantro sprigs.

SERVES 4

4 oz/115 g dried green tea noodles, or the thinnest green noodles you can find

1 oz/30 g butter

1 garlic clove, crushed

pinch of paprika

1 tbsp peanut or corn oil, plus a little extra for cooking the scallops

2 tbsp bottled mild or medium Thai green curry paste

2 tbsp water

2 tsp light soy sauce

2 scallions, finely shredded, and extra scallions, sliced, to garnish

12 fresh scallops, removed from the shells, with shells reserved, if possible (see Note)

salt and pepper

Scallops on Noodles

For an attractive presentation, serve the noodles and scallops on washed and dried scallop shells. You can buy real ones from fish stores, or white porcelain shell-shaped dishes from gourmet kitchen stores. Otherwise, just mound the noodles on a plate and arrange the scallops on them.

• This is an excellent dish to serve at a dinner party, but you have to be organized. You can boil the noodles and make the garlic butter for cooking the scallops ahead of time but, as everything else is done at the last minute, it's a good idea to have your guests seated when you start cooking. You want the scallops to go from the pan to the table as quickly as possible.

• Boil the noodles for about 1 1/2 minutes, until soft, then rinse with cold water and drain well. For any other noodles, follow the package instructions. Drain and set aside. Meanwhile, melt the butter and cook the garlic in it for about 1 minute. Add the paprika and set aside.

• Heat a wok over high heat. Add the oil. Stir in the curry paste, water, and soy sauce and bring to a boil. Add the noodles and stir round to reheat. Stir in the scallions, then remove from the heat and keep warm.

• Heat a ridged, cast-iron grill pan over high heat and brush lightly with a little oil. Add the scallops to the pan and cook for 3 minutes on the first side, then no more than 2 minutes on the second, brushing with the garlic butter, until just cooked (the center shouldn't be totally opaque if cut open). Season with salt and pepper to taste. Divide the noodles into 4 portions and top with 3 scallops each. Garnish with spring onions.

SERVES 4

peanut or corn oil, for deep-frying

9 oz/250 g fresh thin or medium
  Chinese egg noodles

CHICKEN-LIME SALAD

6 tbsp sour cream

6 tbsp mayonnaise

1-inch/2.5-cm piece fresh gingerroot,
  peeled and grated

grated rind and juice of 1 lime

4 skinless, boneless chicken thighs,
  poached and cooled, then cut into
  thin strips

1 carrot, peeled and grated

1 cucumber, cut in half lengthwise,
  seeds removed and sliced

salt and pepper

1 tbsp finely chopped fresh cilantro

1 tbsp finely chopped fresh mint

1 tbsp finely chopped fresh parsley

several fresh basil leaves, torn

Noodle Baskets with Chicken-Lime Salad

If the Noodle Baskets seem too daunting, serve the salad on deep-fried noodles: heat some oil in a wok over to 350–375°F/ 180–190°C. Add 4 oz/ 115 g dried medium rice-flour noodles and deep-fry, stirring, until crisp. Scoop out and drain on paper towels. Repeat with more noodles.

• These impressive-looking baskets are not difficult to shape and cook, but allow yourself a few practice runs first.

• To shape noodle baskets, you can use 2 spider web slotted spoons from an Asian store. Spread the noodles out and place in a mesh spoon. Then place a second mesh spoon over the top and hold the two handles tightly together as you dip the baskets into the oil. Alternatively, you can buy a special set of 2 long-handled wire baskets that clip inside each other, which you can buy at gourmet kitchen stores. Dip the larger wire basket in oil, then line it completely and evenly with one-quarter of the tangled noodles. Dip the smaller wire basket in oil, then position it inside the larger basket and clip it into position.

• Heat 4 inches/10 cm oil in a wok or deep-fat fryer to 350–375°F/180–190°C, or until a cube of bread browns in 30 seconds. Lower the baskets into the oil and deep-fry for 2–3 minutes, or until the noodles are golden brown. Remove the baskets from the oil and drain on paper towels. Unclip the 2 wire baskets and carefully lift up and remove the small one. Use a round-bladed knife, if necessary, to prise the noodle basket from the wire frame. Repeat to make 3 more baskets. Let the noodle baskets cool, then fill and serve, or store in an airtight container for several days.

• Alternatively, serve the salad on noodle cakes: Heat a large skillet over high heat. Add 1 tablespoon of oil and heat until it shimmers. Add half the noodles and press down to form a pancake. At medium heat cook until crusty on the bottom. Slide the cake onto a rimless baking sheet. Invert the skillet over the noodles and flip the baking sheet and skillet, so the noodles drop into the skillet. Add a tablespoon oil to the skillet and continue cooking for 3–4 minutes, until crisp. Drain on paper towels and keep warm in a low oven while cooking the remaining noodles.

• To make the salad, combine the sour cream, mayonnaise, ginger, and lime rind. Gradually add the lime juice to taste. Stir in the chicken, carrot, cucumber, and seasoning to taste. Cover and let chill. Just before serving stir in the herbs and spoon the salad into the noodle baskets.

MAKES 8 EGG ROLLS
3 oz/85 g dried cellophane noodles
1 cooked duck breast, weighing about
   10 oz/300 g
2 tbsp bottled hoisin sauce
2 tbsp bottled plum sauce
1 carrot
3-inch/7.5-cm piece cucumber

6 large lettuce leaves, rinsed and
   dried
8 rice paper skins, about 8 inches/
   20 cm across
generous ¼ cup bean sprouts
2 tbsp very finely chopped fresh mint
1 tbsp very finely chopped fresh
   cilantro, and sprigs, to garnish

DIPPING SAUCE
5 tbsp rice vinegar
2 tbsp honey
1 tbsp toasted sesame oil
½ tsp bottled chili sauce
½-inch/1-cm piece fresh gingerroot,
   peeled and very finely chopped

Vietnamese Egg Rolls

To cook a duck breast, brush a skillet with oil and place over medium–high heat. Add the breast, skin-side down, and cook for 8 minutes, or until crispy. Transfer the duck to an oven preheated to 425°F/220°C and roast for 15–18 minutes for well done.

• These refreshing, uncooked rolls are easiest to assemble if you set up a production line by putting the ingredients on separate plates as they are prepared. Put the noodles in a heatproof bowl, pour over enough lukewarm water to cover, and let soak for 20 minutes, until soft. Alternatively, follow the package instructions. Drain well, then set aside. Meanwhile, remove any skin and fat from the duck and cut the flesh into thin strips, then mix with the hoisin and plum sauces. Peel and coarsely grate the carrot. Cut the cucumber in half lengthwise and scoop out the seeds, then cut each half into short thin sticks. Tightly roll up the lettuce leaves, then slice crosswise into thin shreds.

• Pour ½ inch/1 cm hot water into a dish large enough to hold the rice paper skins. Working with one skin at a time, dip it in the water for 20–25 seconds, until it is soft. Lay the wrapper on a folded dish towel or absorbent mat, but don't worry about patting it dry. Put one-eighth of the lettuce in the center of the bottom third. Top with an equal amount of the noodles, then add some carrot, cucumber, and bean sprouts. Top with one-eighth of the duck mixture and sprinkle with the herbs. Fold in the sides of the rice skin, then roll up. Continue until all the ingredients are used up.

• Stir all the Dipping Sauce ingredients together in a small bowl and serve with the egg rolls.

MAKES 12 WRAPS
3½ oz/100 g dried cellophane noodles
3 tbsp crunchy peanut butter
2 tbsp rice vinegar
1 tbsp oyster sauce
peanut or corn oil (optional)
soy sauce, to taste
4 red radishes, grated
2 carrots, peeled and coarsely grated

1 zucchini, coarsely grated
4 oz/115 g canned corn kernels,
    drained
12 large lettuce leaves, such as
    iceberg, rinsed and dried

DIPPING SAUCE
10 tbsp rice vinegar
4 tbsp honey

2 tbsp toasted sesame oil
½ tsp bottled chili sauce
1-inch/2-cm piece fresh gingerroot,
    peeled and very finely chopped

Lettuce Wraps

Dried cellophane noodles, sold in bunches, are brittle and difficult to separate until they have been soaked. It is easiest to soak a whole bunch, and add any leftovers to salads and soups. They will keep for several days in a plastic bag in the refrigerator.

• This simple Chinese-style dish gets any meal off to a convivial start. Think of it as a do-it-yourself appetizer—you put all the ingredients on the table and your guests assemble their own wraps, rolling lettuce leaves round peanut-flavored noodles tossed with crisp and crunchy salad ingredients. A selection of ingredients for the filling is suggested here, but you can use whatever fresh ingredients you have available. Bean sprouts, sliced scallions, grated red onions, sliced bell peppers, and grated daikon (Japanese white radish), as well as cooked shrimp, all work well.

• Put the noodles in a bowl, pour over enough lukewarm water to cover, and let soak for 20 minutes, until soft. Alternatively, follow the package instructions. Drain and rinse, then cut into 3-inch/7.5-cm lengths.

• Beat the peanut butter, vinegar, and oyster sauce together in a large bowl, adding a little oil to lighten the mixture, if necessary. Toss with the noodles in the bowl to coat, then add soy sauce to taste. Cover and let chill until 15 minutes before you plan to serve. Meanwhile, mix the Dipping Sauce ingredients together in a small bowl, if you are making your own.

• When you are ready to serve, stir in the radishes, carrots, zucchini, and corn and transfer to a serving dish. Each guest takes a lettuce leaf, and uses chopsticks or a fork to add some noodles. Then each individual rolls up the lettuce leaves to enclose the filling (the wraps should look similar to egg rolls).

SERVES 12

2 boneless salmon steaks, weighing about 6 oz/175 g and about ¾ inch/2 cm thick each, skinned

bottled or homemade teriyaki sauce (see Note)

12 large spinach leaves, rinsed and dried with any tough stems removed, or about 36 young spinach leaves

48 long, fresh medium Chinese egg noodles

Noodle-Wrapped Teriyaki Fish

To make your own teriyaki sauce, combine ½ cup each light soy sauce and mirin and 2 tablespoons sugar in a pan. Stir until the sugar dissolves, then bring to a boil and boil until reduced by half. Remove from the heat and let cool. If you can't find fresh egg noodles, boil dried, according to the package, then set aside to dry.

• These bite-size pieces of fish, flavored with Japanese teriyaki sauce, are delicious served with a pre-dinner glass of sparkling wine, and are ideal for entertaining because they can be assembled several hours in advance and chilled until you are ready to steam them just before serving.

• Use a sharp knife to cut the salmon steaks into 1-inch/2.5-cm square pieces, but don't worry if some are irregular: as long as they are about the same size they will steam in the same length of time.

• Brush the top of each fish piece with teriyaki sauce. Working with one spinach leaf at a time, place it on the counter, bottom side up, with the stem end facing you. Place a piece of fish, sauce-side down, in the center of the leaf. Fold the sides inward to overlap, then roll up from the bottom so the fish is enclosed. Continue wrapping the remaining fish pieces. Wrap each spinach package with 2 noodles, from side to side, then repeat with 2 more noodles wrapped at right angles. Have all the dangling loose noodle ends on the bottom, then cut off the excess and press the ends together. Cover and let chill for at least 20 minutes, or up to 8 hours.

• To cook, place a bamboo steamer over a pan of boiling water. Put as many fish packages as will fit in a single layer in the steamer, cover, and let steam for 10 minutes. Serve at once, while you steam any remaining packages.

SERVES 4

12 asparagus tips or spears

toasted sesame oil

4 oz/115 g thin dried Chinese egg
noodles

DRESSING

4 tbsp mirin or sweet sherry

2 tbsp rice vinegar

1 tbsp kecap manis (sweet soy
sauce, see Note)

TO GARNISH

toasted sesame seeds (see Note)

fresh mint leaves

Sesame-Marinated Asparagus with Noodles

Kecap manis is a thick, dark, dark soy sauce used in Indonesian cooking. You will find it in supermarkets, in the gourmet food section or with the other soy sauces, and in Asian food stores. To toast the sesame seeds, stir them round in a dry wok or skillet until they start coloring, then immediately tip them out of the wok.

• The simplicity of this delicate salad showcases the flavor of asparagus in season, but the salad also transforms imported asparagus tips into a light and appetizing first course the rest of the year. This tastes equally good hot or cold, so you can make it ahead and avoid any last-minute rush when you are entertaining. And if you want a slightly more substantial first course, stir in thinly sliced smoked salmon or prosciutto.

• If you are using whole spears, break off any woody, thick ends. Put the asparagus tips or spears in a bowl and rub the sesame oil all over them, then set them aside while you mix all the dressing ingredients together in another bowl. You can carry on with the recipe at this point or cover both bowls and let chill for 1–2 hours.

• Meanwhile, drop the noodles in a pan of boiling water and boil for 3 minutes, until soft. Alternatively, cook the noodles according to the package instructions. Drain, rinse, and drain again. Cover and let chill if you aren't assembling the salad immediately.

• Heat a ridged, cast-iron grill pan over high heat. Add the asparagus tips or spears and charbroil, turning them over occasionally, for 3–5 minutes, depending on the thickness, until they are tender. Add the hot asparagus to the dressing and toss the noodles. Sprinkle with sesame seeds and mint. Serve warm or cool.

MAKES 12 SPOONFULS

2 oz/55 g dried thin buckwheat noodles, or any other thin noodles, such as Japanese somen

4 oz/115 g canned crabmeat (drained weight), any excess liquid squeezed out

2 tbsp very finely chopped fresh parsley

about 2 tbsp fresh lemon juice

salt and pepper

pinch of paprika

A Spoonful of Noodles

For an alternative flavor, toss the noodles with drained, flaked tuna, chopped capers, cilantro, and lime juice to taste. Or, make a Teriyaki Sauce: combine ½ cup each of light soy sauce and mirin and 2 tablespoons sugar in a pan. Stir until the sugar dissolves, boil until reduced by half. Remove from heat and let cool.

• Perfect for a drinks party, this is a simple prepare-ahead canapé that looks stylish served in Chinese soup spoons. These are inexpensive to buy from most Asian food stores—use all one color or a variety of Asian patterns. If you don't have a selection of spoons, however, serve bite-size mounds of the noodle salad on slices of cucumber or radicchio leaves that are firm enough to pick up. This recipe uses Japanese buckwheat noodles, but, in fact, any thin noodle is fine, so you can have even more variety, if you prefer. Green tea noodles look particularly attractive.

• You can make the salad and assemble it in the spoons in advance, but be sure to take them out of the refrigerator 15 minutes before you serve, so the flavors aren't dulled.

• Drop the noodles in a pan of boiling water and boil for 4 minutes, until soft. Alternatively, cook according to the package instructions. Drain, rinse well to remove the excess starch, and drain again.

• Flake the crabmeat into a bowl. Stir in the parsley and 2 tablespoons of the lemon juice, and add salt and pepper and a pinch of paprika. Add a little extra lemon juice, if you like. Toss the noodles with the crab salad.

• Use only a small amount of noodles per spoon. Using a fork, swirl the noodles and crab into a small mound, then place it in the spoon, with any loose ends tucked underneath. Continue until all the ingredients are used.

SERVES 4

3 oz/85 g dried thick rice-flour noodles

generous 3 cups spinach leaves,
    well rinsed and shaken dry

2/3 cup bean sprouts

3½ oz/100 g canned water chestnuts
    (drained weight), sliced

2 hard-cooked eggs, shelled and
    chopped (see Note)

4 bacon slices, rinds removed,
    and cooked until crisp

DEEP-FRIED NOODLES (OPTIONAL)

2 oz/55 g fresh medium Chinese
    egg noodles

peanut oil, for deep-frying

SWEET-AND-SOUR DRESSING

2 shallots, finely chopped

½ cup corn oil

scant ½ cup superfine sugar

2½ tbsp tomato ketchup

2 tbsp rice wine or white wine
    vinegar

1 tbsp Worcestershire sauce

salt and pepper

Spinach Salad with Deep-Fried Noodles

Chopped hard-cooked eggs add richness to this salad. To hard-cook the eggs, put them in a pan and pour over enough boiling water to cover. Bring the water back to a boil, then lower the heat and let simmer for 10 minutes. Drain and rinse under cold water, then shell and chop.

• There are oodles of noodles in this Asian-flavored salad. Soft rice-flour noodles are tossed with spinach leaves to make up the body of the salad, and deep-fried egg noodles add a crunchy topping. Most salad recipes specify tender, young leaves, but this tastes best with slightly older leaves that have more texture.

• Start by soaking the rice-flour noodles in a bowl with enough lukewarm water to cover for 20 minutes, until soft. Alternatively, cook according to the package instructions, drain well, and set aside.

• You can buy bags of already deep-fried noodles in large Asian food stores, but if you want to deep-fry your own, heat enough oil for deep-frying in a wok or pan until a piece of noodle sizzles instantly. Add the noodles and deep-fry for about 1 minute, until they separate and are golden and crisp. Use a slotted spoon or tongs to transfer the noodles to paper towels and let them drain.

• Put all the dressing ingredients in a bowl and beat. Do not mix in a blender or food processor.

• Just before serving, toss the spinach leaves with the rice noodles, bean sprouts, and water chestnuts, then arrange on 4 plates. Top each portion with a good spoonful of the dressing, then add the eggs and crumbled bacon. Sprinkle with the deep-fried noodles.

SERVES 4–6

2 skinless chicken breasts

8 cups water

1 onion, with skin left on, cut in half

1 large garlic clove, cut in half

½-inch/1-cm piece fresh gingerroot, peeled and sliced

4 black peppercorns, lightly crushed

4 cloves

2 star anise

salt and pepper

1 carrot, peeled

1 celery stalk, chopped

3½ oz/100 g baby corn, cut in half lengthwise and chopped

2 scallions, finely shredded

4 oz/115 g dried rice vermicelli noodles

Chicken-Noodle Soup

If you don't have any of the vegetables listed above, other suitable ingredients include drained canned corn kernels, drained canned straw mushrooms, shredded savoy cabbage, and diced red, orange, or yellow bell peppers. Thin Chinese egg noodles also taste good in this soup.

• Chicken-noodle soup can be as homely or as sophisticated as you like. Here it is given an Asian twist, making it a fragrant first course for a Chinese meal. Put the chicken breasts and water in a pan over high heat and bring to a boil. Lower the heat to its lowest setting and let simmer, skimming the surface until no more foam rises. Add the onion, garlic, ginger, peppercorns, cloves, star anise, and a pinch of salt and continue to simmer for 20 minutes, or until the chicken is tender and cooked through. Meanwhile, grate the carrot along its length on the coarse side of a grater so you get long, thin strips.

• Strain the chicken, reserving about 5 cups stock, but discarding any flavoring ingredients. (At this point you can let the stock cool and refrigerate overnight, so any fat solidifies and can be lifted off and discarded.) Return the stock to the rinsed-out pan with the carrot, celery, baby corn, and scallions and bring to a boil. Boil until the baby corn are almost tender, then add the noodles and continue boiling for 2 minutes.

• Meanwhile, chop and add the chicken to the pan and continue cooking for about 1 minute longer until the chicken is reheated and the noodles are soft. Add seasoning to taste.

If you think of noodles only as an ingredient for quickly stir-fried dishes, think again. In Asia, noodles are used just as frequently in delicious salads and soups. Anyone who has traveled throughout the Far East will be familiar with the numerous street vendors selling a seemingly endless variety of soups and salads that are eaten throughout the day. You can adapt this Asian concept to your lifestyle, as the simple recipes in this chapter are suitable for lunch, brunch, supper—or any time. For example, the noodle salads are quick and simple, and feature myriad fresh ingredients as diverse as shellfish, roast duck, and fresh fruit and vegetables, with an intriguing hint of spice. These are for you if traditional meals of meat and two veg don't feature regularly in your life. With a little planning you can transport these dishes to liven up lunch at your desk, or a leisurely weekend picnic.

COOL AND SOOTHING NOODLES

There are few things more comforting than a fragrant bowl of Asian noodle soup. The aromas alone are enough to make you feel good and stimulate your taste buds. The thick and rich coconut-based Thai soups are ideal for meals that can keep you going all day, while clear soups hit the spot when you want something lighter and soothing. The flavors in these recipes are so exciting that snack times and mealtimes need never seem dull again.

SERVES 4

9 oz/250 g dried thin buckwheat
   noodles
2 sheets dried nori seaweed, toasted
   (see Note) and thinly sliced

DIPPING SAUCE

2 cups water
½ tsp dashi granules
½ cup dark soy sauce
up to ¾ cup mirin or sweet sherry

TO SERVE

grated daikon (Japanese white radish)
   or red radish
pink pickled ginger, sliced
scallions, very thinly sliced
wasabi paste

Zaru Soba

Nori seaweed comes in thin sheets from Japanese food stores and health food stores. To crisp it, use a pair of tongs to hold the nori 2–3 inches/5–7.5 cm above a gas flame and toast on both sides. After toasting, use a pair of scissors to cut it very thinly.

• On hot summer days in Japan, this simple chilled buckwheat noodle salad is a popular choice at the numerous noodle bars. It is very easy to assemble, but be sure the noodles are well chilled before you serve them. Traditionally, they are served on a lacquer tray with a bamboo mat surface that lets any excess water drip away. They look just as attractive in a glass bowl set inside a larger bowl of ice.

• Make the Dipping Sauce several hours in advance so it also has time to chill. Bring the water to a boil, then add the dashi granules with the soy sauce and ½ cup of the mirin and stir until the granules dissolve. Taste and add extra mirin, if you like. Let cool, then let chill until quite cold.

• Boil the buckwheat noodles for 3 minutes, until soft. Alternatively, cook according to the package instructions. Drain and rinse in a bowl of cold water, using your hands to swish them round to remove all the excess starch. Put the noodles in a bowl of fresh cold water and let chill until you are ready to serve.

• Divide the Dipping Sauce between individual bowls. Arrange the noodles in a haystack on a mat or on a plate and garnish with toasted nori. Give each guest a plate with the daikon, pickled ginger, scallions, and wasabi arranged separately. Use chopsticks or a fork to add one of the flavorings to a bite of the noodles, then dip the noodles in the sauce.

SERVES 4

½ Peking duck, bought from a
Chinese take-out

1 lb/450 g fresh Hokkien noodles

5 tbsp bottled hoisin sauce

5 tbsp bottled plum sauce

1 small cucumber

4 scallions

Peking Duck Salad

If you can't find Hokkien noodles, any thick noodles, such as udon or many brands of ready-to-use noodles sold in the Asian food sections of supermarkets, are equally suitable. Or boil dried thick Chinese egg noodles for 5 minutes, or according to the package instructions, and use them.

• The flavors of this salad will probably be familiar from the popular Chinese restaurant dish of Peking duck, in which the shredded duck meat is rolled in thin pancakes with thinly sliced cucumber and scallions. Here, however, the pancakes are replaced with the golden yellow, round, fat Hokkien noodles. Since cooking Peking duck, with its crispy skin and meltingly tender flesh, is a 2-day affair, it is probably easier to buy half a Peking duck from a Chinese take-out or supermarket. If that isn't possible, however, roast 2 duck breasts to use instead (see next step.)

• To roast the duck breasts, brush a skillet with oil and place over medium-high heat. Add the breast, skin-side down, and cook for 8 minutes, or until crispy. Transfer the breasts to an over preheated to 425°F/220°C and roast for 15–18 minutes for well done.

• Begin by preparing the Peking duck, or roast and cool duck breasts. Remove the crisp skin and cut it into thin strips, then slice the meat and set both aside separately. The noodles won't need any cooking, but rinse them under lukewarm water to separate them, then let them drain. Meanwhile, mix the hoisin and plum sauces together in a large bowl and add the noodles after any excess water has dripped off. Add the duck skin to the bowl and stir together.

• Cut the cucumber in half lengthwise, then use a teaspoon to scoop out the seeds and cut into half-moon slices and add to the noodles. Next slice the scallions on the diagonal and add to the bowl. Use your hands to mix all the ingredients together so they are coated with the sauce.

• Transfer the noodles to a large platter and arrange the duck meat on top.

SERVES 4
20 cooked jumbo shrimp
20 cooked mussels in their shells
2 oz/55 g oyster mushrooms, wiped
2 scallions, finely sliced
3 kaffir lime leaves, thinly sliced

1 lemon grass stalk, center part only,
  finely chopped
½ red onion, very thinly sliced
3½ oz/100 g dried medium rice-flour
  noodles

THAI COCONUT DRESSING
½ cup creamed coconut
3 tbsp lime juice
1½ tbsp nam pla (Thai fish sauce)
1½ tbsp brown sugar
1–2 fresh red chilies, to taste,
  seeded and thinly sliced
1 small garlic clove, crushed

Thai Fisherman's Catch

Kaffir lime leaves give an unmistakable citrus flavor to many Thai dishes. You will find these bright, shiny leaves in the chiller counter of Asian food stores and some supermarkets. If unavailable, substitute grated lime rind.

• When it comes to convenience, buying shelled and cooked jumbo shrimp and cooked mussels makes this salad very quick and easy to assemble. You can, however, save money by cooking them yourself. To cook the shrimp, bring a pan of water to a boil with several lemon slices, 1 sliced shallot, and 1 tablespoon lightly crushed peppercorns while you prepare the shrimp. To devein the shrimp, shell and remove the heads. Leave the tails intact or remove, as you like. Hold a shrimp with its back upward. Using a small knife, slice along the back, from the head to the tail end. Use the tip of the knife to pull the black vein.

• Reduce the heat to its lowest setting, add the shrimp, and poach them just until they turn opaque and curl. Drain the shrimp and immediately transfer them to a bowl of iced water. When they are cool, pat them dry, and let chill until required.

• To cook the mussels, scrub them well and discard any with broken shells or any open ones that don't close when tapped. Put them in a pan over high heat and shake for 2–4 minutes, until they open. Discard any that remain closed. Cool in iced water, then let chill.

• To make the dressing, stir all the ingredients together in a large bowl until the sugar dissolves. Add the shrimp, mussels, mushrooms, scallions, lime leaves, lemon grass, and red onion, then cover and let chill until required.

• Meanwhile, soak the noodles in a bowl with enough lukewarm water to cover for 20 minutes, until soft. Alternatively, cook according to the package instructions. Drain well.

• To serve, divide the noodles between 4 bowls. Spoon the seafood salad over them, adding any extra dressing.

SERVES 4

7 oz/200 g dried thick Chinese egg
    noodles

3½ oz/100 g snow peas

2 celery stalks

4 cooked skinless chicken thighs

SESAME DRESSING

3 tbsp dark soy sauce

3 tbsp Chinese sesame paste

½ tbsp bottled hoisin sauce

½ tbsp sugar

½–1 tbsp bottled sweet chili cooking
    sauce, to taste

1 tsp rice wine

½ tbsp boiling water

Chicken-Sesame Salad

Make double the quantity of dressing so as to keep a jar in the refrigerator for almost-instant salads. It also tastes good tossed with chilled buckwheat noodles and poached shrimp or salmon. Or, use on a crunchy salad of shredded cabbage with grated carrots, zucchini, and bell peppers.

• This salad tastes best when all the ingredients are well chilled, so make the dressing and boil the noodles several hours in advance. This is also good to serve as part of a party buffet, in which case just double or triple the quantities. Other noodles that work well in this salad include thick rice-flour and buckwheat noodles.

• To make the dressing, whisk the soy sauce, sesame paste, hoisin sauce, sugar, chili sauce, and rice wine together, then whisk in the boiling water and continue whisking until the sugar dissolves. Let the dressing stand until it is cool, then cover and let chill until required.

• Meanwhile, cook the noodles in boiling water for 5 minutes, until soft. Alternatively, cook according to the package instructions. Drain, rinse with cold water to stop the cooking, and drain again. Set aside.

• Use a small, sharp knife to slice the snow peas into thin, lengthwise strips, and cut the celery into thin strips. Use your hands to pull the chicken into thin shreds. If you aren't serving the salad straightaway, cover, and let the chicken and vegetables chill .

• When you are ready to serve, put the noodles, chicken, snow peas, and celery in a large bowl. Toss together so all the ingredients are mixed and pour the dressing on top.

SERVES 4

5 oz/140 g cellophane noodles

2 large mangoes

1 large cucumber

4 tbsp salted peanuts, chopped

2 tbsp toasted sesame seeds
   (see Note)

2 tsp brown sugar

THAI DRESSING

½ cup nam pla (Thai fish sauce)

1 lemon grass stalk, center part only,
   finely chopped

½–1 fresh red chili, to taste, seeded
   and thinly sliced

4 tbsp sugar

4 tbsp thinly sliced fresh mint leaves

2 tbsp finely chopped fresh cilantro

finely grated rind and juice of 1 lime

Crunchy Mango Salad

When you're entertaining, this salad looks stunning presented on a plate lined with a vibrant green banana leaf, which you can buy at Asian food stores. To toast the sesame seeds, stir them round in a dry wok or skillet just until they start coloring. Immediately tip them out of the wok, because they can become burned and bitter-tasting in seconds.

• On hot, sunny summer days when you don't want to cook, this cool and refreshing salad hits the spot. It is also delicious served after a spicy main course instead of dessert. Soak the noodles in a large bowl with enough lukewarm water to cover for 20 minutes, until soft. Alternatively, cook according to the package instructions. Drain well and set aside while you prepare the other ingredients.

• To make the dressing, combine the nam pla, lemon grass, chili, sugar, mint, cilantro, and lime rind and juice in a bowl, stirring until the sugar dissolves. Taste and add a little more of any ingredient to taste until you get a balance you like, then set the bowl aside.

• To prepare the mangoes, put one on a cutting board and slice lengthwise on each side of the seed. Peel and thinly slice the flesh and add it to the dressing, then repeat with the other mango. Cut the cucumber in half lengthwise and use a teaspoon to scoop out the seeds. Then cut into half-moon shapes and add to the mango. Gently stir all the ingredients together. You can either serve the salad at once or cover and let chill for 1–2 hours. Meanwhile, mix the peanuts, sesame seeds, and sugar together, and set aside.

• Divide the noodles between 4 plates and top with the mangoes and cucumbers and a good drizzling of the dressing. Sprinkle the peanut and sesame mixture over the top.

SERVES 4
20–24 large raw unshelled shrimp
2 cups fish stock
pinch of salt
2 cups coconut milk
2 tsp nam pla (Thai fish sauce)
½ tablespoon lime juice
4 oz/115 g dried medium rice-flour
  noodles

⅜ cup bean sprouts
fresh cilantro, chopped, to garnish

LAKSA PASTE
6 fresh cilantro stalks with leaves
3 large garlic cloves, crushed
1 fresh red chili, seeded and chopped
1 lemon grass stalk, center part
  only, chopped

1-inch/2.5-cm fresh gingerroot, peeled
  and chopped
1½ tbsp shrimp paste
½ tsp ground turmeric
peanut oil

Shrimp Laksa

To devein shrimp, shell and remove the heads. Leave the tails intact or remove, as you like. Hold a shrimp with its back upward. Using a small knife, slice along the back, from the head to the tail end. Use the tip of the knife to pull the black vein.

• Buy unshelled shrimp, ideally with heads still intact, because you can add the shells and heads to the simmering stock to intensify the flavor. Shell and devein the shrimp (see Note). Put the fish stock, salt, and the shrimp heads, shells, and tails in a pan over high heat and slowly bring to a boil. Lower the heat and let simmer for 10 minutes.

• Meanwhile, make the Laksa Paste. Put all the ingredients in a food processor and blend. With the motor running, slowly add up to 2 tablespoons oil just until a paste forms. (If your food processor is too large to work efficiently with this small quantity, use a mortar and pestle, or make double the quantity and keep leftovers tightly covered in the refrigerator to use another time.)

• Heat 1 teaspoon oil in a large pan over high heat. Add the paste and stir-fry until it is fragrant. Strain the stock through a strainer lined with cheesecloth. Stir the stock into the Laksa Paste, along with the coconut milk, nam pla, and lime juice. Bring to a boil, then lower the heat, cover, and let simmer for 30 minutes.

• Meanwhile, soak the noodles in a large bowl with enough lukewarm water to cover for 20 minutes, until soft. Alternatively, cook according to the package instructions. Drain and set aside.

• Add the shrimp and bean sprouts to the soup and continue simmering just until the shrimp turn opaque and curl. Divide the noodles between 4 bowls and ladle the soup over, making sure everyone gets an equal share of the shrimp. Garnish and serve.

SERVES 4

4 oz/115 g dried cellophane noodles

5 cups chicken or vegetable stock

1 lemon grass stalk, crushed

½-inch/1-cm piece fresh gingerroot, peeled and very finely chopped

2 fresh kaffir lime leaves, thinly sliced

1 fresh red chili, or to taste, seeded and thinly sliced

2 skinless, boneless chicken breasts, thinly sliced

scant 1 cup coconut cream

2 tbsp nam pla (Thai fish sauce)

about 1 tbsp fresh lime juice

scant ½ cup bean sprouts

green part of 4 scallions, finely sliced

fresh cilantro leaves, to garnish

Thai Chicken-Coconut Soup

Put bean sprouts in the refrigerator as soon as you get them home so they remain crisp and crunchy, and always observe the use-by date. Discard any that become brown and soggy, but if they are only slightly limp a soaking in cold water for 15 minutes should revive them.

• Typical of the soups sold by street vendors throughout Thailand, this is a rich and satisfying meal in a bowl. Enjoy it at any time of the day.

• Soak the dried noodles in a large bowl with enough lukewarm water to cover for 20 minutes, until soft. Alternatively, cook according to the package instructions. Drain well and set aside.

• Meanwhile, bring the stock to a boil in a large pan over high heat. Lower the heat, add the lemon grass, ginger, lime leaves, and chili and let simmer for 5 minutes. Add the chicken and continue simmering for an additional 3 minutes, or until the flesh is poached. Stir in the coconut cream, nam pla, and 1 tablespoon lime juice and continue simmering for 3 minutes. Add the bean sprouts and scallions and let simmer for an additional 1 minute. Taste and gradually add extra nam pla or lime juice at this point, if you like. Remove and discard the lemon grass stalk.

• Divide the noodles between 4 bowls. Bring the soup back to a boil, then add the soup to each bowl. The heat of the soup will warm the noodles. To garnish, sprinkle with cilantro leaves.

SERVES 4

½ oz/15 g dried Chinese wood ear
    mushrooms

4 oz/115 g dried thin Chinese egg
    noodles

2 tsp arrowroot or cornstarch

4 cups vegetable stock

2-inch/5-cm piece fresh gingerroot,
    peeled and sliced

2 tbsp dark soy sauce

2 tsp mirin or sweet sherry

1 tsp rice vinegar

4 small bok choy, each cut in half

salt and pepper

snipped fresh Chinese or ordinary
    chives, to garnish

Chinese Mushroom Soup

When reconstituted, dried Chinese wood ear mushrooms develop a delicate, leaflike texture and a mahogany color, which makes them a popular ingredient in Chinese soups. Cloud ear mushrooms are smaller, but look similar and can be used in this soup.

• This is a warm, soothing soup. The ginger adds a subtle, spicy flavor, and is reputed to relieve headaches and heavy colds. Put the dried wood ear mushrooms in a heatproof bowl and pour over enough boiling water to cover, then let them stand for 20 minutes, or until they are tender. Meanwhile, boil the noodles for 3 minutes, until soft. Alternatively, cook according to the package instructions. Drain well and rinse with cold water to stop the noodles cooking, and set aside.

• Strain the mushrooms through a strainer lined with a dish towel and reserve the liquid. Put the arrowroot in a wok or large pan and gradually stir in the reserved mushroom mixture. You can leave the mushrooms whole, or slice them, depending on how large they are. Add the vegetable stock, sliced ginger, soy sauce, mirin, rice vinegar, mushrooms, and bok choy and bring the mixture to a boil, stirring constantly. Lower the heat and let simmer for 15 minutes.

• Add salt and pepper to taste, but remember that soy sauce is salty so you might not need any salt at all—taste first. Use a slotted spoon to remove the pieces of ginger.

• Divide the noodles between 4 bowls, then spoon the soup over and garnish with chives.

SERVES 4

4 cups vegetable stock

1 stalk lemon grass, center part only,
    finely chopped

1 tsp tamarind paste

pinch of dried red pepper flakes, or
    to taste

5 oz/140 g thin green beans, cut into
    1-inch/2.5-cm pieces

1 tbsp light soy sauce

1 tsp brown sugar

juice of ½ lime

9 oz/250 g firm tofu, drained and cut
    into small cubes

2 scallions, sliced on the diagonal

2 oz/55 g enoki mushrooms, hard
    end of the stalks cut off

14 oz/400 g fresh udon noodles

Monk's Soup

Delicate, thin enoki mushrooms, from Japan, can be found in the vegetable section of some large supermarkets and Asian food stores. They have long, thin stems with tiny caps on top, and add a slightly crunchy texture to soups and salads. Their flavor is less earthy than that of other mushrooms.

• Despite its name, there isn't anything self-sacrificing about this vegetarian feast with a refreshing sweet-and-sour flavor and a hint of heat from the red pepper flakes. Look for vacuum packs of udon noodles in the Asian food section of supermarkets, but if you can't find any you can use "straight to wok" noodles or cooked thick Chinese egg noodles, which are just as suitable.

• Put the vegetable stock in a large pan with the lemon grass, tamarind paste, and red pepper flakes and bring to a boil, stirring until the tamarind dissolves. Lower the heat and add the green beans and let simmer for 6 minutes. Add the soy sauce, brown sugar, and lime juice. Taste at this point and stir in more sugar, lime juice, or red pepper flakes to get the balance of sweet, sour, and heat you like.

• Stir in the tofu and scallions and continue simmering for just 1–2 minutes longer, or until the green beans are tender, but still with a bit of bite, and the tofu is warm. Add the enoki mushrooms. Pour boiling water over the udon noodles to separate them, then divide them between 4 large bowls. Divide the soup between the bowls. The heat of the soup will warm the noodles.

SERVES 4

4 cups fish or vegetable stock

1 large garlic clove

½ tsp light soy sauce

4 salmon fillets, 5 oz/140 g each,
     skinned

peanut or corn oil, for broiling

5 oz/140 g dried ramen or thin
     Chinese egg noodles

generous 2 cups baby spinach leaves

4 scallions, chopped

TO SERVE

⅔ cup bean sprouts

1 fresh green chili, seeded and sliced

fresh cilantro leaves

TERIYAKI GLAZE

2½ tbsp sake

2½ tbsp dark soy sauce

2 tbsp mirin or sweet sherry

½ tbsp brown sugar

½ garlic clove, very finely chopped

¼-inch/0.5-cm piece fresh gingerroot,
     peeled and very finely chopped

Salmon Ramen

Soy sauce is one of the most commonly used flavorings in Asian cooking. Made from fermented soybeans, it has a salty flavor, and you will find both light and dark varieties. Light soy sauce is the saltier of the two.

• It will be like having a noodle bar at home when you make this Japanese dish that is a cross between a soup and a salad in a bowl. Dried ramen noodles are the ones you find wrapped together in tight bundles, often labeled simply as "stir-fry noodles." But, if you can't find any, just substitute any Japanese or Chinese egg noodles. While you heat the broiler to high, bring the stock to a boil with the garlic clove and soy sauce in one pan, and bring another pan of water to a boil for cooking the noodles.

• Mix the ingredients for the glaze together and brush one surface of each salmon fillet with the glaze. Lightly brush the broiler rack with oil and broil the salmon fillets for 4 minutes on one side only. The flesh should flake easily and the center should remain a bright pink. Remove from the broiler and set aside.

• Boil the noodles for 3 minutes, until soft. Alternatively, cook according to the package instructions. Drain and rinse. Remove the garlic from the stock, then bring the stock back to a boil. Drop in the spinach leaves and scallions and let them boil until the leaves are just wilted. Use a slotted spoon to remove the spinach and scallions and divide them between 4 large bowls.

• Divide the noodles between the bowls, then add a salmon fillet to each. Carefully pour the boiling stock into each bowl. Sprinkle with bean sprouts, chili slices, and cilantro leaves.

When it comes to quick cooking, noodles and woks are an unbeatable combination. Stir-fried noodle dishes are easy, satisfying, and can be on the table in a flash. The recipes in this chapter are as appealing to the eye as they are to the palate, which makes them ideal for easy, informal entertaining, as well as family suppers. These are one-pot meals that mean you spend less time cooking—and less time washing up!

Although stir-frying itself is quick, you will have to spend a bit of time preparing the ingredients. Most of the chopping and slicing, however, can be done while the noodles soak or boil. If you plan to make stir-fries regularly, it is a good idea to stock up on prepared vegetables, bottled sauces, and ready-to-cook noodles. When chopping ingredients for stir-fries, the aim is to cut

NOODLES IN A FLASH

similarly textured vegetables, meat, poultry, and fish to the same size so they are all ready to eat at the same time. Add the thickest ingredients first, then progress to the quicker-cooking ones, and you will soon appreciate how foolproof stir-frying is. A wok is ideal to use for the recipes in this chapter, because it heats quickly and the large surface area means ingredients cook quickly. A large, heavy-bottom skillet can also be used.

The simple golden rules of stir-frying are to heat the wok or skillet before you add the oil, and to heat the oil before you start adding ingredients. These two steps should prevent small pieces of food sticking and burning.

SERVES 4

7 oz/200 g dried medium or thick
    rice-flour noodles

2 tbsp brown sugar

1 tbsp tamarind paste, or 2 tbsp
    lemon juice

1 tbsp hot water

4 tbsp salted peanuts

1 tbsp peanut or corn oil

1 shallot, finely chopped

10½ oz/300 g small shelled shrimp,
    thawed if frozen

2 large eggs, beaten

2 oz/55 g firm tofu (drained weight),
    crumbled with your fingers

2 tbsp nam pla (Thai fish sauce)

1 scallion, finely chopped

⅓ cup bean sprouts

large pinch white sugar

pinch of dried red pepper flakes,
    to taste

chopped fresh cilantro, to garnish

Pad Thai

Tofu, made from soy milk, features in many Asian recipes as a vegetarian source of protein, and comes with a firm or soft texture. Asian food stores also sell cooked tofu, which can be added with the noodles. Keep tofu refrigerated and observe the use-by date.

• Pad Thai is the ultimate Thai street food that makes a meal for any time of the day. Soak the noodles in enough lukewarm water to cover for 20 minutes, until soft. Alternatively, cook according to the package instructions. Drain and set aside. Meanwhile, mix the brown sugar, tamarind paste, and hot water together, stirring until the tamarind dissolves, then set aside.

• Heat a wok or large skillet over high heat. Add the peanuts without any oil and dry-fry, stirring constantly, until they just turn golden. Immediately tip the peanuts out of the wok, then finely chop them and set aside.

• When you are ready to start cooking, reheat the wok over high heat. Add the oil and heat until it shimmers. Add the shallot and stir-fry for 30 seconds–1 minute until it starts to color. Add the shrimp and stir-fry for an additional 30 seconds. Lower the heat to medium, push the shallot and shrimp to one side of the wok, pour the eggs into the wok, and stir until they are scrambled and firmly set. (You don't want softly scrambled breakfast eggs for this.)

• Turn the heat back up to high. Add the tofu to the wok and stir it round to give it color. Add the noodles, tamarind mixture, nam pla, scallion, bean sprouts, white sugar, and red pepper flakes. Use 2 large forks to mix all the ingredients together and continue stir-frying for about 2 minutes longer to warm through. Sprinkle with cilantro, and serve.

SERVES 4

7 oz/200 g dried rice vermicelli
noodles

1 tbsp mild, medium, or hot curry
paste, to taste

1 tsp ground turmeric

6 tbsp water

2 tbsp peanut or corn oil

½ onion, very thinly sliced

2 large garlic cloves, thinly sliced

3 oz/85 g broccoli, cut into very small
florets

3 oz/85 g green beans, trimmed,
and cut into 1-inch/2.5-cm pieces

3 oz/85 g pork fillet, cut in half
lengthwise, and then into thin
strips (see Note), or skinless,
boneless chicken breast, thinly
sliced

3 oz/85 g small cooked shelled
shrimp, thawed if frozen

2 oz/55 g Chinese cabbage or
romaine lettuce, thinly shredded

¼ Thai chili, or to taste, seeded
and thinly sliced

2 scallions, light green parts only,
thinly shredded

fresh cilantro, to garnish

Singapore Noodles

For really thin slices of pork fillet that cook quickly, wrap the piece of fillet in plastic wrap, and put it in the freezer for 20 minutes before you slice it. Partially freezing the fillet makes it easier to slice—a technique that works with beef and lamb fillets.

• Make this take-out favorite as mild or spicy hot as you like, depending on the curry paste you use and how much fresh red chili you include. Soak the noodles in enough lukewarm water to cover for 20 minutes, until soft. Alternatively, cook according to the package instructions. Drain and set aside until required. While the noodles are soaking, put the curry paste and turmeric in a small bowl, and stir in 4 tablespoons of the water, then set aside.

• Heat a wok or large skillet over high heat. Add the oil and heat until it shimmers. Add the onion and garlic and stir-fry for 1 minute, or until the onion softens. Add the broccoli and beans to the wok with the remaining 2 tablespoons water and continue stir-frying for an additional 2 minutes. Add the pork and stir-fry for 1 minute. Add the shrimp, cabbage, and chili to the wok and continue stir-frying for an additional 2 minutes, until the meat is cooked through and the vegetables are tender, but still with a little bite. Scoop out of the wok and keep warm.

• Add the scallions, noodles, and curry paste mixture to the wok. Use 2 forks to mix the noodles and onions together, and continue stir-frying for about 2 minutes, until the noodles are hot and have picked up a dark golden color from the turmeric. Return the other ingredients to the wok and continue stir-frying and mixing for 1 minute. Garnish with fresh cilantro.

SERVES 4

1 large carrot

9 oz/250 g dried thick Chinese egg
noodles

2 tbsp peanut or corn oil

2 large garlic cloves, very finely
chopped

1 large red onion, cut in half and
thinly sliced

½ cup vegetable stock or water

2 tbsp bottled chili bean sauce

2 tbsp Chinese sesame paste

1 tbsp dried Szechuan peppercorns,
roasted and ground (see Note)

1 tsp light soy sauce

2 small bok choy or other Chinese
cabbage, cut into quarters

Szechuan Noodles

Szechuan peppercorns are sold in supermarkets and Asian food stores. Dry-fry over high heat until fragrant, tip them out of the skillet and set aside to cool, then grind with a mortar and pestle or in a spice grinder. The powder will keep almost indefinitely in an airtight container.

• This is a gutsy, robust dish for anyone who likes a blast of chili heat in their food. Chili bean sauce often features in Szechuan cooking and it adds a savory, hot flavor. You will find it with other Chinese sauces in some supermarkets and most Asian food stores. Peel the carrot and cut off both ends, then grate it lengthwise on the coarsest side of a grater to make long, thin strips. Set the carrot strips aside.

• Cook the noodles in a pan of boiling water for 4 minutes, until soft. Alternatively, cook according to the package instructions. Drain and rinse with cold water to stop the cooking, then set aside.

• Heat a wok or large skillet over high heat. Add the oil and heat until it shimmers. Add the garlic and onion and stir-fry for 1 minute. Add the vegetable stock, chili bean sauce, sesame paste, ground Szechuan peppercorns, and soy sauce and bring to a boil, stirring to blend the ingredients together. Then add the bok choy quarters and carrot strips and continue stir-frying for 1–2 minutes, until they are just wilted. Add the noodles and continue stir-frying, using 2 forks to mix all the ingredients together. Serve the noodles when they are hot.

SERVES 4

9 oz/250 g dried medium Chinese egg noodles

2 tbsp peanut or corn oil

1 onion, thinly sliced

4 boneless chicken thighs, skinned and cut into thin strips

1 carrot, peeled and cut into thin half-moon slices

1 red bell pepper, cored, seeded, and finely chopped

3½ oz/100 g canned bamboo shoots (drained weight)

generous ⅜ cup cashews

SWEET-AND-SOUR SAUCE

½ cup water

1½ tsp arrowroot

4 tbsp rice vinegar

3 tbsp brown sugar

2 tsp dark soy sauce

2 tsp tomato paste

2 large garlic cloves, very finely chopped

½-inch/1-cm piece fresh gingerroot, peeled and very finely chopped

pinch of salt

Sweet-and-Sour Noodles with Chicken

The clear, glossy shine on these noodles comes from using arrowroot. If you don't have any, however, cornstarch will thicken the sauce just as effectively, albeit with less of a shine. Always stir water or cooking liquid into the thickening agent to prevent lumps.

• Bottled sweet-and-sour sauces are a quick option for when you don't want to spend much time in the kitchen. When you aren't rushed, however, try the sauce in this recipe. It is thinner and less cloying than many of the commercial sauces. Cook the noodles in a large pan of boiling water for 3 minutes, until soft. Alternatively, cook according to the package instructions. Drain, rinse, and drain again, then set aside. Meanwhile, to make the sauce, stir half the water into the arrowroot, and set aside. Stir the remaining sauce ingredients and the remaining water together in a small pan and bring to a boil. Stir in the arrowroot mixture and continue boiling until the sauce becomes clear, glossy, and thick. Remove from the heat and set aside. (At this point, you can let the sauce cool and store it in the refrigerator for up to 1 week.)

• Heat a wok or large skillet over high heat. Add the oil and heat it until it shimmers. Add the onion and stir-fry for 1 minute. Stir in the chicken, carrot, and bell pepper and continue stir-frying for about 3 minutes, or until the chicken is cooked through. Add the bamboo shoots and cashews and stir them round to lightly brown the nuts. Stir the sauce into the wok and heat until it starts to bubble. Add the noodles and use 2 forks to mix them with the chicken and vegetables.

SERVES 4

2 tsp mirin or sweet sherry

1½ tsp light soy sauce

1 tsp toasted sesame oil

½ tsp salt

4 oz/115 g cooked boneless
   lamb or chicken

2 oz/55 g snow peas

1 small red onion

1 red bell pepper

1 carrot

9 oz/250 g fresh udon or ramen
   noodles

generous 2 cups bean sprouts

2 tbsp chopped fresh cilantro

TO GARNISH

rolled omelet slices (see Note)

pink pickled ginger, sliced or
   shredded

toasted sesame seeds

Hot Wok Noodles

For omelet slices, beat 1 large egg with ½ teaspoon water. Heat 1 teaspoon oil in a skillet over high heat. Pour in the egg and tilt the skillet so it covers the bottom. Lower the heat and cook until set. Slide the omelet out, roll up, and slice thinly.

• This is a dish for easy entertaining—assemble all the ingredients in advance, then set them aside until it's time to tip them into a hot wok for just 1–2 minutes' stir-frying. As the cooking is so quick, have your guests seated before you heat the wok. Combine the mirin, soy sauce, sesame oil, and salt in a large bowl, stirring until the salt dissolves. Set this mixture aside while you prepare the other ingredients, adding each one to the bowl as it is ready.
• To toast the seasame seeds, stir the then round in a dry wok or skillet just until they start coloring. Then immediately tip the seeds out of the wok, because they can become burned and bitter-tasting in seconds.
• Remove any excess fat from the lamb, or any skin from the chicken, then thinly slice the flesh. Cut the snow peas into thin, long strips. Cut the onion in half crosswise, then slice into half-moon shapes. Seed and thinly slice the red bell pepper. Peel and coarsely grate the carrot.
• Add the noodles and bean sprouts to the bowl, then use your hands to toss and coat all the ingredients. You can now cover and chill the bowl for up to 2 hours, or cook at once.
• When it's time to cook, heat a wok or large skillet over high heat. Add the noodle mixture and stir-fry for 3 minutes, or until all the ingredients are hot and the vegetables are just tender. Stir in the cilantro. Divide between 4 plates, then top with omelet slices, pickled ginger, and toasted sesame seeds.

SERVES 4

10½ oz/300 g boneless sirloin steak, thinly sliced

9 oz/250 g dried thick Chinese egg noodles

2 tbsp peanut or corn oil

8 oz/225 g fresh asparagus spears, woody ends cut off and chopped

2 large garlic cloves, finely chopped

½-inch/1-cm piece fresh gingerroot, peeled and finely chopped

½ red onion, thinly sliced

4 tbsp beef or vegetable stock

1½ tbsp rice wine

2–3 tbsp bottled oyster sauce

toasted sesame seeds, to garnish (see Note)

MARINADE

1 tbsp light soy sauce

1 tsp toasted sesame oil

2 tsp rice wine

Beef Noodles with Oyster Sauce

Toasting sesame seeds enhances their flavor and gives them an attractive light golden-brown color. Stir the seeds round in a dry wok or skillet just until they start coloring. Immediately tip them out of the wok, because they can become burned and bitter-tasting in seconds.

• This dish is best when you let the beef marinate, but if you are in a hurry, add the marinade ingredients to the wok when you stir in the stock. To make the marinade, stir the ingredients together in a nonmetallic bowl. Stir in the steak so all the slices are coated, then set aside to marinate for at least 15 minutes. Meanwhile, boil the noodles in a pan of boiling water for 4 minutes, until soft. Alternatively, cook according to the package instructions. Drain, rinse, and drain again, then set aside.

• When you are ready to stir-fry, heat a wok or large skillet over high heat. Add 1 tablespoon of the oil and heat. Add the asparagus and stir-fry for 1 minute. Tip the beef and marinade into the wok, standing back because it will splutter, and continue stir-frying until the beef is cooked to your taste, about 1½ minutes for medium. Remove the beef and asparagus from the wok and set aside.

• Heat the remaining oil and stir-fry the garlic, ginger, and onion for about 1 minute, until the onion is soft. Add the stock, rice wine, and oyster sauce and bring to a boil, stirring. Return the beef and asparagus to the wok, along with the noodles. Use 2 forks to mix all the ingredients together and stir round until the noodles are hot. Sprinkle with toasted sesame seeds.

SERVES 4

6 tbsp water

3 tbsp soy sauce

1 tbsp cornstarch

3 tbsp peanut or corn oil

4 boneless chicken thighs, skinned
and chopped

1-inch/2.5-cm piece fresh gingerroot,
peeled and finely chopped

2 large garlic cloves, crushed

2 celery stalks, thinly sliced

3½ oz/100 g white mushrooms,
wiped and thinly sliced

4 noodle baskets made with fresh
medium Chinese egg noodles,
to serve

Chicken Chow Mein Baskets

Deep-fried rice noodles can replace the baskets. Heat enough oil for deep-frying in a wok over high heat to 350–375°F/180–190°C. Add 4 oz/115 g dried medium rice-flour noodles and deep-fry, stirring, until crisp (about 30 seconds). Scoop out and drain on paper towels. Repeat with more noodles.

• Chicken chow mein is traditionally served with deep-fried noodles (see Note), but here the stir-fried chicken and vegetable mixture is presented in crisp, deep-fried noodle baskets.

• Stir the water and soy sauce into the cornstarch in a small bowl and set aside.

• Heat a wok or large skillet over high heat. Add 2 tablespoons of the oil and heat until it shimmers. Add the chicken and stir-fry for about 3 minutes, or until it is cooked through. Use a slotted spoon to remove the chicken from the wok. Add the remaining oil, then add the ginger, garlic, and celery and stir-fry for 2 minutes. Add the mushrooms and continue stir-frying for an additional 2 minutes. Remove the vegetables from the wok and add them to the chicken.

• Pour the cornstarch mixture into the wok and bring to a boil, stirring until it thickens. Return the chicken and vegetables to the wok and reheat in the sauce. Place the noodle baskets on 4 plates and divide the chicken mixture between them.

SERVES 4

9 oz/250 g dried medium Chinese egg noodles

2 tbsp peanut or corn oil

1 large garlic clove, crushed

1 fresh green chili, seeded and sliced

1 tbsp Chinese five-spice powder

2 skinless, boneless chicken breasts, cut into thin strips

2 green bell peppers, cored, seeded, and sliced

4 oz/115 g broccoli, cut into small florets

2 oz/55 g green beans, trimmed and cut into 1½-inch/4-cm pieces

5 tbsp vegetable or chicken stock

2 tbsp bottled oyster sauce

2 tbsp soy sauce

1 tbsp rice wine or dry sherry

2/3 cup bean sprouts

Chicken and Green Vegetables

Bottled oyster sauce is a thick sauce often used in Chinese cooking. It is made from a concentration of oysters cooked with soy sauce, but it doesn't taste fishy. Instead, it adds a rich, sweet flavor to dishes. It is sold in most supermarkets, as well as Asian food stores.

• This recipe is easily adapted to include whatever vegetables you have to hand. Asparagus tips, yard-long beans, and bok choy are all suitable, as are frozen peas. (Add them straight from the freezer as soon as the chicken is cooked through and stir-fry for about 1 minute before you add the other ingredients.) Cook the noodles in a pan of boiling water for 4 minutes, until soft. Alternatively, cook according to the package instructions. Drain, rinse, and drain again, then set aside.

• Heat a wok or large skillet over high heat. Add 1 tablespoon of the oil and heat until it shimmers. Add the garlic, chili, and five-spice powder and stir-fry for about 30 seconds. Add the chicken and stir-fry for 3 minutes, or until it is cooked through. Use a slotted spoon to remove the chicken from the wok and set aside.

• Add the remaining oil to the wok and heat until it shimmers. Add the bell peppers, broccoli, and beans and stir-fry for about 2 minutes. Stir in the stock, oyster sauce, soy sauce, and rice wine and return the chicken to the wok. Continue stir-frying for about 1 minute, until the chicken is reheated and the vegetables are tender, but still firm to the bite. Add the noodles and bean sprouts and use 2 forks to mix all the ingredients together.

SERVES 4

1 lb/450 g boneless lamb leg steaks, trimmed and cut into thin strips

9 oz/250 g dried medium rice-flour noodles

2 tbsp peanut or corn oil

½–1 fresh red chili, to taste, cored, seeded, and thinly sliced

2 red bell peppers, cored, seeded, and thinly sliced

4 tbsp bottled black bean and garlic sauce

4 tbsp chopped fresh mint

3 tbsp sesame seeds, toasted (see Note)

MARINADE

3 tbsp dark soy sauce

2 tbsp brown sugar

1½ tbsp rice wine

2 tsp toasted sesame oil

Lamb with Red Bell Peppers

Most of a chili's heat is from a compound called capsicin, found in the seeds and membranes. If you like a fiery-hot taste, do not remove all the seeds. For a milder taste, seed the chili, using the tip of a small knife to scrape out the seeds. To toast the sesame seeds, stir them round in a dry wok or skillet just until they start coloring. Immediately tip them out of the wok, because they can become burned and bitter-tasting in seconds.

• You don't have to marinate the lamb, but if you have the time, the mixture adds an extra sweetness to the meat that contrasts well with the chili. To make the marinade, mix the soy sauce, sugar, rice wine, and oil together in a nonmetallic bowl. Add the lamb and stir round so all the pieces are coated, then set aside to marinate for 30 minutes, or cover and refrigerate for up to 1 day. Meanwhile, soak the noodles in a bowl of lukewarm water for 20 minutes, until soft. Alternatively, cook according to the package instructions. Drain well and set aside.

• When ready to start cooking, heat a wok or large skillet over high heat. Add the oil and heat it until it shimmers. Add the red chili and stir it round for 30 seconds, then add the red bell peppers and continue stir-frying for 1 minute.

• Spoon the lamb and any marinade into the wok, standing back because it will splutter. Stir- fry for 2 minutes. Stir in the black bean and garlic sauce and cook until all of the liquid evaporates, the lamb is just pink in the center if you cut a piece, and the bell peppers are tender, but still firm to the bite.

• Add the noodles and use 2 forks to mix all the ingredients together. When the noodles are hot, stir in the mint and toasted sesame seeds.

SERVES 4

2 oz/55 g dried Chinese cloud ear
   mushrooms
3½ oz/100 g baby corn, halved
   lengthwise
2 tbsp honey
1 tbsp tamarind paste (see Note)
4 tbsp boiling water
2 tbsp dark soy sauce

1 tbsp rice vinegar
2 tbsp peanut or corn oil
1 large garlic clove, very finely
   chopped
½-inch/1-cm piece fresh gingerroot,
   peeled and very finely chopped
½ tsp dried red pepper flakes, or
   to taste

12 oz/350 g pork fillet, thinly sliced
4 scallions, thickly sliced on the
   diagonal
1 green bell pepper, cored, seeded,
   and sliced
9 oz/250 g fresh Hokkien noodles
chopped fresh cilantro, to garnish

Sour-and-Spicy Pork

Dark brown, sticky tamarind paste is used in Asian recipes to add a sour flavor. It is sold in Indian and other Asian food stores, but if you can't find any, omit the water above and stir 1 tablespoon lime juice into the honey.

• For really thin slices of pork fillet that cook quickly, wrap the piece of fillet in plastic wrap, and put it in the freezer for 20 minutes before you slice it.

• Soak the mushrooms in enough boiling water to cover for 20 minutes, or until they are tender. Drain them well, then cut off and discard any thick stems, and slice the cups if they are large. Meanwhile, bring a large pan of lightly salted water to a boil, add the baby corn, and blanch for 3 minutes. Drain the corn and run them under cold running water to stop the cooking, then set aside. Put the honey and tamarind paste in a small bowl and stir in the water, stirring until the paste dissolves. Then stir in the soy sauce and rice vinegar and set aside.

• Heat a wok or large skillet over high heat. Add 1 tablespoon of the oil and heat until it shimmers. Add the garlic, ginger, and red pepper flakes and stir-fry for about 30 seconds. Add the pork and continue stir-frying for 2 minutes.

• Add the remaining oil to the wok and heat. Add the scallions, bell pepper, mushrooms, and baby corn, along with the tamarind mixture, and stir-fry for an additional 2–3 minutes, until the pork is cooked through and the vegetables are tender, but still firm to the bite. Add the noodles and use 2 forks to mix all the ingredients together. When the noodles and sauce are hot, sprinkle with cilantro.

Don't let your cooking fall into a rut, with the same dishes featuring regularly. Look no further than the noodle recipes in this chapter for everyday inspiration. These are filling, after-work, one-dish meals for sharing with friends or family—they are flavorsome and easy. Versatile Asian noodles can take the place of potatoes, rice, or pasta on your plate.

These innovative recipes use a wide range of main ingredients with plenty of fresh vegetables. The only thing extra you will need is a green salad, if you wish. You'll find recipes suitable for vegetarians and meat-eaters alike.

This is the chapter to turn to during the week when there isn't time for leisurely, complicated cooking. Several of these recipes save you time by using good-quality stir-fry sauces. Get in the habit of picking up a couple of jars every time you shop, along

MAKING A MEAL OUT OF NOODLES

with several packages of dried Asian noodles, and you'll always be able to prepare a quick, delicious meal. It's also a good idea to stock up on the Asian sauces and oils that add so much flavor to mealtimes, such as soy sauce, sesame oil, oyster sauce, plum sauce, and hoisin sauce, so you can rustle up a quick, unusual meal when friends stop by.

Children and adults alike will enjoy these dishes. The modern recipes give a new dimension to regular favorites like chops, steaks, and ground meat without any fuss.

SERVES 4
2 oz/55 g dried Chinese mushrooms
4 oz/115 g firm tofu, drained
2 tbsp bottled sweet chili sauce
    (see Note)
2 tbsp peanut or corn oil
2 large garlic cloves, chopped

½-inch/1-cm piece fresh gingerroot,
    peeled and finely chopped
1 red onion, sliced
½ tbsp Szechuan peppercorns,
    lightly crushed
2 oz/55 g canned straw mushrooms
    (drained weight), rinsed

vegetable stock
1 star anise
pinch of sugar
soy sauce, to taste
4 oz/115 g cellophane noodles

A Firepot of Mushrooms and Tofu

Read the label carefully when you buy sweet chili sauce, and make sure you get one that is suitable for cooking use. Some, which tend to be a clear, bright red, are only dipping sauces. If you can't find any, use chili bean sauce instead.

• Thin, translucent cellophane noodles make this into a one-pot vegetarian meal. Soak the mushrooms in enough boiling water to cover for 20 minutes, or until soft. Cut the tofu into bite-size chunks and stir with the chili sauce until coated, then let marinate.

• Just before you are ready to start cooking, strain the soaked mushrooms through a strainer lined with a paper towel, reserving the soaking liquid. Heat the oil in a medium-size ovenproof casserole or large skillet with a lid. Add the garlic and ginger and stir them round for 30 seconds. Add the onion and peppercorns and keep stirring until the onion is almost tender. Add the tofu, the soaked mushrooms, and canned mushrooms and stir round carefully so the tofu doesn't break up.

• Add the reserved strained mushroom soaking liquid to the wok with just enough vegetable stock or water to cover. Stir in the star anise and a pinch of sugar with several dashes of soy sauce. Bring to a boil, then reduce the heat to the lowest setting, cover, and let simmer for 5 minutes. Add the noodles to the wok, re-cover and simmer for an additional 5 minutes, or until the noodles are tender. The noodles should be covered with liquid, so add extra stock at this point, if necessary. Use a fork or wooden spoon to stir the noodles into the other ingredients. Add soy sauce to taste.

SERVES 2

4 oz/115 g thin dried Chinese egg
    noodles
2 scallions, sliced on the diagonal
about 5 tbsp peanut or corn oil
1 large onion, sliced

1 large steak, such as sirloin,
    weighing about 10½ oz/300 g
    in total and ½ inch/1 cm thick
salt and pepper
6 tbsp bottled Thai red curry paste
2 oz/55 g block creamed coconut,
    dissolved in ⅓ cup boiling water

Steak with Crisp Noodle Cakes

High-quality sirloin steak is specified here because of the cooking time. An alternative would be to use boneless chicken breast.

• Boil the noodles for 3 minutes, or according to the package instructions, then drain well and set aside until they are no longer wet. Do not rinse them, because you want the starch to stick them together. Put in a bowl, add the scallions, and toss.

• Heat a large skillet over high heat. Add 1 tablespoon of the oil and heat until it shimmers. Add half the noodles and press down firmly to form a flat pancake. Lower the heat to medium and cook for 4 minutes, or until crusty on the bottom. Slide the noodle cake onto a rimless baking sheet. Invert the skillet over the noodles and flip both the baking sheet and skillet, so the noodles drop into the skillet. Add another tablespoon oil to the skillet and continue cooking for 3–4 minutes, until crisp. Drain on paper towels, then keep warm in a low oven while you cook the remaining noodles.

• Wipe out the skillet and add 1 tablespoon oil. Add the onion and cook for about 3 minutes, until soft. Season the steak with salt and pepper, add to the skillet and cook for 2 minutes. Turn over the steak, add the red curry paste, and stir in the creamed coconut. Let the steak cook in the sauce for an additional 2 minutes for medium-rare, then remove. Boil the sauce for 1–2 minutes, until it thickens.

• Thinly slice the steak on the diagonal, arrange on the noodle cakes, and spoon the sauce over.

SERVES 4

9 oz/250 g dried medium rice-flour
    noodles
about 2 tbsp peanut or corn oil
5½ oz/150 g bottled black bean
    and garlic sauce
4 scallions, finely chopped
fresh parsley sprigs, to garnish

SPICY MEATBALLS

1 cup lean fresh ground beef
1 oz/30 g chestnut mushrooms,
    wiped and chopped
½–1 fresh red chili, to taste, seeded
    and chopped
1-inch/2.5-cm piece fresh gingerroot,
    peeled and finely chopped

1 tbsp bottled oyster sauce
½ tbsp bottled chili sauce, or to taste
fresh parsley sprigs, to garnish
salt and pepper (optional)

Noodles and Meatballs

Cook a small amount of the meatball mixture and taste before you roll it into meatballs. This way you can determine if it requires seasoning with salt and pepper without eating the raw meat. For lighter meatballs, use half ground pork and half ground beef.

• East meets West in this spicy version of spaghetti and meatballs. Start by soaking the noodles in enough lukewarm water to cover for 20 minutes, until soft. Alternatively, cook according to the package instructions. Drain well, then set aside.

• Meanwhile, make the meatballs. Put all the meatball ingredients in a bowl and mix together using your hands. Add salt and pepper, if necessary (see Note). To shape, lightly wet your hands with cold water, then roll the mixture into 16 walnut-size balls. Cover the meatballs with plastic wrap and let chill for up to 1 day, or proceed with cooking now. Heat 1 tablespoon oil in a large skillet with a lid over medium-high heat. Add as many meatballs as will fit in a single layer without overcrowding and cook until evenly brown. Continue with any remaining meatballs, adding a little extra oil, if necessary. Tip the excess fat out of the skillet and return all the meatballs. Add the black bean and garlic sauce, turn the heat to medium, cover the skillet, and let simmer for 10–15 minutes, until the meatballs are cooked through.

• Remove the meatballs and sauce and keep warm. Wipe out the skillet and reheat. Add about 1 tablespoon oil, add the scallions, and stir round for 1 minute, or until they soften. Add the noodles and reheat. Transfer the noodles to 4 plates, top with the meatballs and sauce, and garnish with parsley sprigs.

SERVES 4

7 oz/200 g dried thick rice-flour
   noodles

16 very thin slices of lime

4 banana leaves, about 14 x 8 inches/
   35 x 20 cm, cut without the central
   stems

4 tuna steaks, about 5 oz/140 g each
   and ¾ inch/2 cm thick

salt and pepper

COCONUT-CILANTRO PASTE

2 oz/55 g block creamed coconut,
   chopped

1 oz/30 g fresh cilantro leaves and
   stalks, coarsely chopped

2 garlic cloves, chopped

1-inch/2.5-cm piece fresh gingerroot,
   peeled and grated

½ tbsp sugar

pinch of dried red pepper flakes,
   or to taste

2 tbsp nam pla (Thai fish sauce)

juice of ½ lime

Tuna and Noodles in Banana Leaves

If you cannot find banana leaves, use a double thickness of waxed paper. It's worth making a double quantity of the paste because it will remain fresh in a container in the refrigerator for a few days. You can also use it to marinate chicken, pork, and beef before broiling.

• Just as the French cook seafood in paper packages to keep it moist and capture the flavor, the Thais use banana leaves. You can buy these in Asian food stores. To make the Coconut-Cilantro Paste, put the creamed coconut, cilantro, garlic, ginger, sugar, and red pepper flakes in a food processor and process until all the ingredients are finely chopped. With the motor running, add the nam pla and lime juice, and process to a thick paste.

• Meanwhile, soak the noodles in enough lukewarm water to cover for 20 minutes, until soft. Alternatively, cook according to the package instructions. Drain well and set aside. Arrange 4 slices of lime along the center of each piece of banana leaf. Season each fish fillet with salt and pepper and place on top of the lime slices, then spread a quarter of the paste over each. Add a quarter of the noodles alongside the fish, then fold up each banana leaf like a package to seal in all the juices. Use a piece of kitchen string to close the banana-leaf package securely. Marinate for 30 minutes.

• When you are ready to cook, place a steamer large enough to hold the 4 fish packages in a single layer over a pan of boiling water, without letting the water touch the bottom of the steamer. Add the fish packages and let steam for 15 minutes. Open 1 package to make sure the fish is cooked through and flakes easily. Remove the string, then serve the packages for each guest to open their own.

SERVES 4

4 boneless chicken breasts, about
    6 oz/175 g each, with or without
    skin, as you wish
about 4 tbsp bottled teriyaki sauce
peanut or corn oil
cucumber fans, to garnish

SESAME NOODLES

9 oz/250 g dried thin buckwheat
    noodles
1 tbsp toasted sesame oil
2 tbsp toasted sesame seeds
2 tbsp finely chopped fresh parsley
salt and pepper

Teriyaki Chicken with Sesame Noodles

These noodles also go well with broiled cod, salmon, tuna, or mackerel, but let the fish marinate for 30 minutes at the most. Broil the fish, brushing with the sauce, until the flesh flakes easily. To toast the sesame seeds, stir them in a dry wok or skillet just until they start coloring. Then immediately tip them out of the wok.

• This is a good prepare-ahead dish, so there is very little to do when the time comes to cook. Let the chicken marinate while you are out all day, then you just have to take it out of the refrigerator when you start heating the broiler. Using a sharp knife, score each chicken breast diagonally across 3 times and rub all over with teriyaki sauce. Set aside to marinate for at least 10 minutes, or cover and let chill all day.

• When you are ready to cook the chicken, preheat the broiler to high. Bring a pan of water to a boil, add the buckwheat noodles, and boil for 3 minutes, until soft. Alternatively, cook according to the package instructions. Drain and rinse well in cold water to stop the cooking and remove excess starch, then drain again.

• Lightly brush the broiler rack with oil. Add the chicken breasts, skin-side up, and brush again with a little extra teriyaki sauce. Broil the chicken breasts about 4 inches/10 cm from the heat, brushing occasionally with extra teriyaki sauce, for 15 minutes, or until cooked through and the juices run clear.

• Meanwhile, heat a wok or large skillet over high heat. Add the sesame oil and heat until it shimmers. Add the noodles and stir round to heat through, then stir in the sesame seeds and parsley. Finally, add salt and pepper to taste.

• Transfer the chicken breasts to plates and add a portion of noodles to each.

SERVES 4

1 tbsp peanut or corn oil

finely grated rind and juice of 1 large
    lemon

4 cod or haddock steaks, about
    5 oz/140 g each, skinned

paprika, to taste

salt and pepper

SPICED NOODLES

9 oz/250 g dried medium Chinese
    egg noodles

1 tbsp peanut or corn oil

2 garlic cloves, chopped

1-inch/2.5-cm piece fresh gingerroot,
    peeled and finely chopped

2 tbsp very finely chopped fresh
    cilantro roots

1 tbsp kecap manis (sweet soy
    sauce, see page 22)

1 Thai chili, seeded and finely
    chopped

1 tbsp nam pla (Thai fish sauce)

Cod with Spiced Noodles

Nam pla, or Thai fish sauce, adds an intense savory flavor to many noodle dishes. It smells fishy in the bottle, but when it is cooked the fishiness is less noticeable. You will find it with other Asian sauces in supermarkets and Asian food stores.

• If you think of broiled fish as boring, think again! These spicy, zingy noodles perk up any fish, so don't limit yourself to the ones suggested here—broiled mackerel is also delicious with these. Preheat the broiler to high. While the broiler is heating, put the noodles in a pan of boiling water and boil for 3 minutes, until soft. Alternatively, cook according to the package instructions. Drain, rinse with cold water to stop the cooking, and drain again, then set aside. (If you want to cook the noodles in advance, toss them with a teaspoon or so of sesame oil and set aside.)

• Mix 1 tablespoon of the oil with the lemon juice and brush over one side of each fish steak. Sprinkle with the lemon rind and a dusting of paprika and add a little salt and pepper. Lightly brush the broiler rack with oil, then broil the fish, about 4 inches/10 cm from the heat, for 8–10 minutes, until the flesh flakes easily.

• Meanwhile, heat a wok or large skillet over high heat. Add 1 tablespoon oil and heat until it shimmers. Add the garlic and ginger and stir-fry for about 30 seconds. Add the cilantro and kecap manis and stir round. Add the noodles and give a good stir so they are coated in the kecap manis. Stir in the chopped chili and nam pla.

• Serve each broiled fish steak on a bed of noodles.

SERVES 4

9 oz/250 g dried thick Chinese egg
    noodles, or Chinese wholemeal
    egg noodles
1 lb/450 g pork fillet, thinly sliced
1 tsp sugar
1 tbsp peanut or corn oil
4 tbsp rice vinegar
4 tbsp white wine vinegar

4 tbsp bottled hoisin sauce
2 scallions, sliced on the diagonal
about 2 tbsp garlic-flavored corn oil
2 large, fresh garlic cloves thinly
    sliced (from garlic with a tight-
    fitting papery skin, that has been
    stored at room temperature)
chopped fresh cilantro, to garnish

Hoisin Pork with Garlic Noodles

For really thin slices of pork fillet that cook quickly, wrap the piece of fillet in plastic wrap, and put it in the freezer for 20 minutes before you slice it. Partially freezing the fillet makes it easier to slice—a technique that works with beef and lamb fillets.

• Garlic lovers will adore these noodles, as they pack a real punch. They also taste good with broiled steaks. Start by boiling the noodles for 3 minutes, until soft. Alternatively, cook according to the package instructions. Drain well, rinse under cold water to stop the cooking, and drain again, then set aside.

• Meanwhile, sprinkle the pork slices with the sugar and use your hands to toss together. Heat a wok or large skillet over high heat. Add the oil and heat until it shimmers. Add the pork and stir-fry for about 3 minutes, until the pork is cooked through and is no longer pink. Use a slotted spoon to remove the pork from the wok and keep warm. Add both vinegars to the wok and boil until they are reduced to about 5 tablespoons. Pour in the hoisin sauce with the scallions and let bubble until reduced by half. Add to the pork and stir together.

• Quickly wipe out the wok and reheat. Add the garlic-flavored oil and heat until it shimmers. Add the garlic slices and stir round for about 30 seconds, until they are golden and crisp, then, before they become too brown and develop a bitter taste, use a slotted spoon to scoop them out of the wok and set aside.

• Add the noodles to the wok and stir them round to warm them through. Divide the noodles between 4 plates, top with the pork and onion mixture, and sprinkle cooked garlic slices and cilantro, if you like.

SERVES 4

4 oz/115 g dried thin cellophane
    noodles

2 lb/900 g selection of vegetables,
    such as carrots, baby corn,
    cauliflower, broccoli, snow peas,
    onions

6 eggs

4 scallions, chopped on the diagonal

salt and pepper

2½ tbsp peanut or corn oil

3½ oz/100 g canned bamboo shoots,
    drained

7 oz/200 g bottled sweet-and-sour
    sauce

Sweet-and-Sour Vegetables on Noodle Pancakes

Cellophane noodles come in large bunches that can be difficult to separate until after they have been soaked. If they are tied with a piece of string, leave the string in place until after you drain them and are ready to cut them into smaller pieces.

• Soak the noodles in enough lukewarm water to cover and let stand for 20 minutes, until soft. Alternatively, cook according to the package instructions. Drain them well and use scissors to cut into 3-inch/7.5-cm pieces, then set aside.

• Meanwhile, peel and chop the vegetables as necessary. It doesn't really matter what vegetables you use, or how varied the selection is, but they should all be cut to about the same size, so they will all be tender, but still firm to the bite, when you finish stir-frying.

• Beat the eggs, then stir in the noodles, the scallions, and salt and pepper to taste. Heat an 8-inch/20-cm skillet over high heat. Add 1 tablespoon oil and swirl it round. Pour in a quarter of the egg mixture and tilt the skillet so it covers the bottom. Lower the heat to medium and cook for 1 minute, or until the thin pancake is set. Flip it over and add a little extra oil, if necessary. Continue cooking until the pancake is set. Keep warm in a low oven while you make 3 more pancakes.

• After you've made 4 pancakes, heat a wok or large skillet over high heat. Add 1½ tablespoons oil and heat until it shimmers. Add the thickest vegetables, such as carrots, first, and stir-fry for 30 seconds. Gradually add the remaining vegetables and bamboo shoots. Stir in the sauce and stir-fry until all the vegetables are tender and the sauce is hot. Spoon the vegetables and sauce over the pancakes and sprinkle with cilantro.

SERVES 4

4 lamb steaks or boneless loin chops

peanut or corn oil

salt and pepper

fresh mint or cilantro sprigs, to
garnish

lime wedges, to serve

HERB NOODLES

juice of 1 lime

1 tbsp nam pla (Thai fish sauce)

½ tbsp bottled sweet chili coooking
sauce

1 tsp brown sugar

½ tbsp sesame oil

9 oz/250 g dried thick Chinese egg
noodles

5 tbsp finely chopped mint leaves

5 tbsp finely chopped cilantro leaves

Lamb Steaks with Herb Noodles

Supermarkets now stock a steady supply of fresh herbs throughout the year, such as the cilantro and mint used in this recipe. Only buy herbs with a clean, fresh fragrance and bright green color. Do not buy any that look wilted or are tinged with brown.

• This is one of those dishes that defines "quick cooking"—it can be on the table within 15 minutes of walking into the kitchen. And, as an added bonus, it is equally good served hot straight from the stove or left to cool for tepid summer eating. Start by mixing together the flavorings for the noodles. Put the lime juice, nam pla, sweet chili sauce, brown sugar, and sesame oil in a small bowl and beat together, then set aside.

• Heat a large ridged cast-iron grill pan or skillet over high heat. Lightly brush the steaks or chops with oil on both sides and season with salt and pepper. Add them to the pan and cook for about 6 minutes for rare, or 10 minutes for well done, turning the meat over once.

• Meanwhile, boil the noodles for 3 minutes, until soft. Alternatively, cook according to the package instructions. Drain well and immediately transfer to a large bowl. Add the lime juice mixture and toss together, then stir in the chopped fresh herbs.

• Serve the lamb steaks with the noodles on the side. Sprinkle with extra herbs, if you like, and lime wedges for squeezing over.

SERVES 4

9 oz/250 g dried thick rice-flour
   noodles

1 tbsp cornstarch

3 tbsp soy sauce

1½ tbsp rice wine

1½ tsp sugar

1½ tsp toasted sesame oil

1½ cups lean fresh ground pork

1½ tbsp peanut or toasted sesame oil

2 large garlic cloves, finely chopped

1 large fresh red chili, or to taste,
   seeded and thinly sliced

3 scallions, finely chopped

finely chopped fresh cilantro or
   parsley, to garnish

Ants Climbing a Tree

Made from glutinous rice, yeast, and water, rice wine is used to flavor many traditional Chinese dishes, especially noodle dishes. It has a rich, mellow flavor and is available in supermarkets, as well as Asian food stores. Store it tightly sealed at room temperature.

• If the idea of eating ants doesn't appeal, fear not—the "ants" in the dish are actually nothing more than small amounts of cooked ground pork that are said to look like ants climbing up the noodles. Children love this for the novelty of the title, but adults are more appreciative of the rich, savory flavors. Soak the rice noodles in enough lukewarm water to cover for 20 minutes, until soft. Alternatively, cook according to the package instructions. Drain well and set aside.

• Meanwhile, put the cornstarch in another large bowl, then stir in the soy sauce, rice wine, sugar, and sesame oil, stirring so no lumps form. Add the ground pork and use your hands to toss the ingredients together without squeezing the pork; set aside to marinate for 10 minutes.

• Heat a wok or large skillet over high heat. Add the oil and heat until it shimmers. Add the garlic, chili, and scallions and stir round for about 30 seconds. Tip in the ground pork together with any marinade left in the bowl and stir-fry for about 5 minutes, or until the pork is no longer pink. Add the noodles and use 2 forks to mix together. Sprinkle with the chopped herbs and serve.

Index